PRESENCE & PURPOSE

THE MISSION OF JESUS
IN THE BOOK OF ACTS

ISBN 978-1-0877-4915-0
Item 005833732
Dewey Decimal Classification Number: 242
Subject Heading: DEVOTIONAL LITERATURE / BIBLE STUDY AND TEACHING / GOD

Printed in the United States of America

Student Ministry Publishing
Lifeway Resources
One Lifeway Plaza
Nashville, Tennessee 37234

We believe that the Bible has God for its author; salvation for its end; and truth, without any mixture of error, for its matter and that all Scripture is totally true and trustworthy. To review Lifeway's doctrinal guideline, please visit www.lifeway.com/doctrinalguideline.

Unless otherwise noted, all Scripture quotations are taken from the Christian Standard Bible®, Copyright © 2017 by Holman Bible Publishers. Used by permission. Christian Standard Bible® and CSB® are federally registered trademarks of Holman Bible Publishers.

publishing team

Director, Student Ministry
Ben Trueblood

Manager, Student Ministry Publishing
John Paul Basham

Editorial Team Leader
Karen Daniel

Writer
Jennifer Dixon

Content Editor
Stephanie Cross

Production Editor
Brooke Hill

Cover Design
Kaitlin Redmond

Graphic Designer
Shiloh Stufflebeam

TABLE OF CONTENTS

INTRO

Have you ever gone to hang out with your friend and found her in the middle of a Netflix binge? She's been watching the show for a while, but you have just jumped in the middle of an episode in the middle of a season. You don't know the characters, the setting, or the plot. Still, you find yourself drawn in: The story is compelling. The characters are real. The twists and turns are shocking and gripping. When this happens, you go home and start watching from season one, episode one, right?

In a similar way, that's where we find ourselves when it comes to the church. There have been two thousand seasons of episodes before our season. So to learn what happened before we entered the story, we go to the very first episode. For our "show," this means starting where the church as we know it began—the book of Acts.

Through stories of bravery, impossible odds, and new beginnings, you'll find answers to questions like: "Where did it all begin?" "What makes someone a Christian?" and "What is God's purpose for my life?" Though you may not realize it until you dig deep into the book of Acts, these real-life accounts from the early church heavily inform and influence Christianity today.

As you study, the events from two thousand years ago will seem less like ancient history and more like vital truth for your life right now. These stories are compelling, the characters were real, and the pages of the Bible are filled with shocking and gripping truths. The people in Acts faced bullies, uncertainty, racism, exclusion, fear, and temptation to follow the crowd. But they persevered, and their love for Jesus spread the gospel through all the world—even to you today.

This devotional is designed not only to inform you of the past, but also to guide you into the future. Over the next thirty days, expect to be challenged in your own faith and to grow in your knowledge of God and His unique purpose for you as you study the book of Acts.

GETTING STARTED

This devotional contains thirty days of content, broken down into sections. Each day is divided into three elements—discover, delight, and display—to help you explore Scripture.

discover |

This section helps you examine the passage in light of who God is and determine what it says about your identity in relationship to Him. Included here is the daily Scripture reading, key verses, along with illustrations and commentary to guide you as you learn more about God's Word.

delight |

In this section, you'll be challenged by questions and activities that help you see how God is alive and active in every detail of His Word and your life.

display |

Here's where you take action. Display calls you to apply what you've learned through each day.

> **Each day also includes a prayer activity at the conclusion of the devotion.**

Throughout the devotional, you'll also find other resources to help you connect with the topic, such as Scripture memory verses, activities, and articles that help you go deeper into God's Word.

section 1

SETTING THE STAGE

While the book of Acts isn't the first in the Bible, it is another story of beginnings—the beginning of the church. Many significant events happened before this point—most important is Jesus's life, death, and resurrection. In this, Jesus, the Son of God, proved He conquered death and sin. And when Jesus preached about His kingdom, He told His disciples to believe Him. Then Jesus called them to do the same thing: tell others about His kingdom and call them to believe in Him. But He didn't leave them without help. In the very beginning of this book of beginnings, Jesus promised the Holy Spirit, who became the catalyst for the rest of the book of Acts, leading the disciples to the ends of the earth with the message that all who believe in Jesus will be saved from sin and death.

What's Next?

discover |

READ ACTS 1.

"But you will receive power when the Holy Spirit has come on you, and you will be my witnesses in Jerusalem, in all Judea and Samaria, and to the ends of the earth." —Acts 1:8

After His resurrection, Jesus made many public appearances, proving He is God and the Messiah. He continued teaching people about God's kingdom up until the day He ascended back into heaven. His final words while physically present on earth are recorded in this first chapter of Acts. His words promise us His continued presence through the Holy Spirit and give our lives a purpose—to be His witnesses.

The Holy Spirit is of great benefit to followers of Jesus. He remains with us and does not abandon us in our task of being witnesses. He reminds us about what Jesus taught and continues teaching us (see John 14:26). The Holy Spirit will work in the lives of the people we talk to, convicting them of their sin (see John 16:8). He is also a guide for truth and a constant reminder of Jesus's love (see John 16:13). God never sends His people out on a task alone—He is always with us.

A witness is someone who simply retells what they saw or experienced. They don't have to complete a class or pass a test. They just have to have experienced something others haven't and report about it. The disciples had a personal experience with Jesus. It may not be like the personal experience you have (or can have) with Jesus, but He offers Himself to anyone who will come to Him in faith. The disciples certainly didn't know what all they were getting into with Jesus, but they followed Him anyway. What He said, they did. What He taught, they took in. The process for you will be similar—get to know Jesus, do what He says, study His words and seek to understand them, and you also will become a witness to the amazing work of Jesus.

delight |

Does having someone present who truly loves you make a difference for you? How so?

Are you experiencing Jesus? Do you have anything to report to others about the things you have gone through that show others what Jesus is like?

display |

I don't know where you are in your relationship with Jesus. Don't feel bad if you can't come up with anything to share with others. Here is something really simple you can do to point people to Jesus: get to know someone who wants to be a part of your life. Jesus sent His Holy Spirit to draw you to Him. Come near to Him. Ask Him to teach you and be your comfort and guide. If you do, He has promised that you will have experiences with Him that are definitely worth sharing with others.

Name one girl who you can develop a relationship with that can result in you telling her about Jesus.

Thank God for Jesus. Thank God for the Holy Spirit. Thank Him for loving you enough to send you a Savior and a companion. Tell God about where you feel you are in your journey with Him. Thank Him for past experiences with Jesus (if you have them) and ask to experience Him now and in the future.

DAY 2

The Spirit Came

discover |

READ ACTS 2.

Peter replied, "Repent and be baptized, each of you, in the name of Jesus Christ for the forgiveness of your sins, and you will receive the gift of the Holy Spirit." —Acts 2:38

Remember what Jesus promised His disciples they would receive after He left? He said they'd receive the Holy Spirit. In today's reading, it happened—and it happened in a BIG way! The Spirit came with the sound of a violent wind. Some say tornado winds approaching is one of the most terrifying sounds in nature. People have compared it to a freight train, a rushing waterfall, or a nearby jet engine. Imagine that was the sound heard as the Spirit came. Next, "tongues like flames of fire" appeared (v. 3). These flames split and rested on each disciple, showing that each one received the Spirit in a unique and powerful way.

Having heard the ruckus, a crowd appeared. The disciples began preaching about Jesus. The sermon Peter gave may be unlike any sermon you've heard. It certainly didn't persuade people to come to Jesus for reasons you've heard before like forgiveness of sins or unconditional love. Peter preached to a group of devout Jews. Peter showed them that Jesus is the fulfillment of what their people had long been waiting for. There is an infinite amount of reasons to trust in Jesus, and when you share with others about Him, there are many reasons a person should place their faith in Him.

Notice the people's response to the disciples: some thought they were drunk, while others believed. Even with the Holy Spirit demonstrating a supernatural experience, some just wouldn't believe. But the Spirit working in the disciples compelled them to share regardless of the response by the audience.

delight |

Think back to the times you've heard the news of Jesus preached. What reasons to trust in Him do you personally find the most convincing?

What has your response to the news of Jesus been like? Have you repented and believed, or do you have doubts?

display |

After the spectacular coming of the Holy Spirit, we don't see Him come again this way for anyone else; but there is evidence we can find of the Holy Spirit's dwelling in each of us. It won't look like flames or sound like a tornado, but it'll be an internal change, which is just as powerful. It will compel us to share Jesus with others and to be more concerned about obeying Jesus than how people react to the message.

Write one sentence about how you know the Holy Spirit lives in you. If you aren't sure, write a prayer asking God to help you have confidence in Him and His plan for your life.

Thank God that His Spirit works in ordinary people such as yourself. Talk to God if you have any doubts about the Spirit living in you. Ask Him to make His Spirit known to you and to help you follow His leading. If you haven't committed your life to Jesus and want to, tell God about your desires.

Presence and Purpose

The Lame Will Walk

discover |

READ ACTS 3.

God raised up his servant and sent him first to you to bless you by turning each of you from your evil ways. —Acts 3:26

Some time had passed between the end of Acts 2 and the beginning of Acts 3. The disciples were learning to live out their new reality as Holy Spirit vessels. Notice that Peter and John were still going to the temple to pray even though they could talk to God whenever because He resided in them through His Spirit. As you'll see throughout the book of Acts, just because you have the Holy Spirit doesn't mean you have all the answers to how to live out the Christian life.

While they were at the temple, the disciples encountered a man who couldn't walk and believed what he needed most was money. Since he was unable to walk, providing for himself in those times would've been extremely difficult. Desk jobs were not plentiful back then. Peter and John confessed that they had no silver or gold, but as servants of Christ, they did not pass this man by. They told him to walk "in the name of Jesus Christ" (v. 6), and he did! He immediately began walking and praising God. He was overjoyed that his life was changed forever, and he was ready to call Jesus his God.

A crowd grew around to see what all the commotion was about. This crowd wanted to know Peter and John's secret power, and they told the people about Jesus. They didn't take full credit, but told the people Jesus was readily available to be their Savior as well.

delight |

Do you believe God cares for your physical and spiritual needs? How does the Scripture today demonstrate He does care for both?

When you succeed at something, where do you give the credit? Can you acknowledge areas of your success that can only be attributed to God?

display |

God cares for you. Maybe you've heard that a lot and it feels old, or maybe you haven't heard it enough—but it's true. He wants to help you. He is able to cause incredible healing to all areas of your life. He cares for your spirit, your body, your mind, your emotions, and your thoughts. So, talk to Him for the help you need no matter what your issue is. You can start by writing out any ways you need His help in these areas:

Spirit

Body

Mind

Emotions

Thoughts

Thank God for caring for you as a whole person—not just your spirit. Talk to Him about getting His help in all areas of your life. Praise God for the successes you've had in life. Confess times you've neglected to thank Him in the past for your successes.

Ordinary to Extraordinary

discover |

READ ACTS 4.

*When they observed the boldness of Peter and John and realized
that they were uneducated and untrained men, they were amazed
and recognized that they had been with Jesus. —Acts 4:13*

A group of religious leaders was curious about Peter and John. No one could deny that the man walking before them was once unable to walk. They obviously had miraculous powers, and these leaders wanted to know where their power came from. Peter and John answered them with confidence that it was all because of Jesus. They knew full well these men would not like their answer.

If any group should've intimidated Peter and John, it would've been this group of religious leaders. They had power and influence among the people and the Roman government, but Peter and John responded to their threats with boldness. This boldness was a big change for Peter and John. It's hard to believe, but back before Jesus was crucified, both Peter and John abandoned Him (see Matt. 26:56). Because of peer pressure, Peter even denied being friends with Jesus (see Matt. 26:69-75; Mark 14:66-72).

These men didn't start out as extraordinary spokesmen for Jesus. They had been intimidated in the past, and it took time with Jesus, witnessing His death and resurrection, and being filled with the Holy Spirit before these changes took place.

delight |

What is your definition of extraordinary?

What steps do you think you need to take to become someone extraordinary for Jesus?

display |

Becoming a girl who is considered "changed by Jesus" will mean taking similar steps to those Peter and John took. Being changed by Jesus takes time spent with Him, reading and studying His teachings, and mimicking His attitude and behavior. It will also take belief in Jesus's death and, more importantly, His resurrection. If Jesus did not rise from the dead, then our faith is useless. Our faith is in Someone who is still alive and working. Lastly, we need the Spirit to come dwell in our lives. He directs our desires to long for the things God has for us. So, what steps have you taken to be changed by Him? Where has He taken ordinary things about you and turned them into extraordinary things? Write out a summary of where you think you are in your faith in Jesus.

Talk to God about the changes in your life since learning about Jesus. Tell Him if you do or don't see any changes. If you don't, then ask for His help. Praise Him that He still changes people like you today.

Presence and Purpose

Can't Stop God

discover |

READ ACTS 5.

"So in the present case, I tell you, stay away from these men and leave them alone. For if this plan or this work is of human origin, it will fall; but if it is of God, you will not be able to overthrow them. You may even be found fighting against God." They were persuaded by him. —Acts 5:38-39

The early church was seeing some truly amazing things! A man and his wife dropped dead after lying to God (see vv. 1-10). Sick people were being healed. People tormented by demons were being liberated. Thousands of people were joining the church. And the religious leaders of the day were at their wit's end. They wanted the disciples' compelling teaching about Jesus to stop attracting their followers.

The religious leaders had the apostles arrested, but even the jail cell could not stop God's plan for these men. An angel freed them, and the Jewish leaders were forced to re-evaluate their approach and try to find a different way to stop the apostles. They called a meeting and had everyone show up, thinking, "maybe we can intimidate these men by outnumbering them." Not likely. The disciples refused to budge.

A well-respected teacher, Gamaliel, offered some wise advice: If these men were from God, there was nothing they could do to stop them, and they would find themselves fighting against God. If these men were not from God, then the movement they began would end when they died. So what did the Sanhedrin decide? To let them live. Their decision reveals that there was a sense among these leaders that God was at work in the disciples.

delight |

Who intimidates you? Why?

How might being confident that the presence of God is with you help when facing a bully?

display |

Some girls aren't going to like what you are doing when you decide to follow Jesus. They may try to intimidate you to stop, but remind yourself that if God is at work, then no bully on earth can stop it. Remind yourself that you are on the team of the all-powerful God. You have chosen to align yourself with God, and no person can stop what He wants to do in your life and through you.

Think about the girl who intimidates you most. Write her name here and commit to praying for her.

On an index card, write the words: "God is all-powerful. He is with me. No one can stop God's work in me or through my life." Keep this card with you as a reminder to daily choose to follow Jesus, no matter what others do or say.

Maybe you have already been intimidated by others so much so that you abandoned God. Talk to Him about times you've succumbed to intimidation. Ask God to remind you of His presence when you feel threatened. Thank Him that the work He has for you will not be stopped by any person or situation.

DAY 6

Help Needed

discover |

READ ACTS 6.

*Now Stephen, full of grace and power, was performing great
wonders and signs among the people. —Acts 6:8*

The Christian church was growing by leaps and bounds. Consequently,
the apostles were being overworked. There were people with physical
needs that were being neglected. The apostles realized, like many of us
do, that we can not complete God's work on our own. We all need help,
even those who have the ability to speak in multiple languages, heal
sicknesses, cast out demons, and stand up to the meanest bullies. If the
apostles needed help, so does anyone else who decides to join God in
His mission.

One helper in particular, Stephen, was given more attention in the
Scriptures than the others. He was said to be "full of grace and power
[and] was performing great wonders and signs among the people" (v.
8). Anyone could recognize that Stephen was gifted by God to do
incredible things, and yet here, we see him given the great and noble
task to . . . wait tables. Did the thought cross your mind that waiting
tables was beneath a man gifted at performing great wonders and
signs? Well, the apostles didn't, and neither did Stephen. Even if a task
may be completed by any able-bodied person, that doesn't mean it is
beneath the most gifted of us all.

There is no level of Christian superiority that excuses anyone from
serving people in need. Service to others is a valuable, worthwhile, and
essential part of doing God's work here on earth.

delight |

Do you ever get frustrated when you are forced into a situation where you realize you can't do something by yourself and have to ask for help? Dig deep into why you might feel this frustration.

How could you make time to serve others? How might you show appreciation to those who are serving you?

display |

Meeting the physical needs of those less fortunate is emphasized over and over in the Bible. James 1:27 tells us that to care for orphans and widows is considered pure religion to God. In other words, when we care for others in need, we are doing the most authentic act of devotion to God. Think about how you can find ways to serve others. You may not have the resources on your own, but talk to your family or youth group to find ways you can work together to help someone in need.

Here's an idea to get you started: Invite over some godly girls you know. Ask them each to think about at least two other girls (outside of your group) who might need some encouragement. Grab some index cards (or pretty cards!), markers, and colored pens. When you get together, write out notes of encouragement to the two girls you thought of. Then, as a group, pray over each name. Be sure to give the girls the notes of encouragement you wrote!

Show your gratitude to God for being the kind of sovereign King who cares about helping those in need. He has allowed you to be part of His plans to help those in need. Ask God to give you a heart for service. Ask Him to help you see ways you can serve others and show appreciation to those around you who serve you.

ACTS 4:13

MEMORY VERSE

When they observed the
boldness of Peter and John
and realized that they were
uneducated and untrained
men, they were amazed and
recognized that they had
been with Jesus.

Love Worth Dying For

discover |

READ ACTS 7.

While they were stoning Stephen, he called out: "Lord Jesus, receive my spirit!" He knelt down and cried out with a loud voice, "Lord, do not hold this sin against them!" And after saying this, he died. —Acts 7:59-60

Up to this point in the story, it seems as though the disciples of Jesus were invincible. Yet here in Acts 7, we see they weren't. Today's reading is a solemn reminder that physical death comes to all of us. There is a fate worse than death, however, and that is to face God without having our sins removed through the work of Jesus. It is a fate so terrible that Stephen did not wish it on his worst enemies.

Stephen spoke to his accusers about the history of the Israelites. He wanted them to realize that the temple and the law of Moses were not more important than an actual relationship with God Himself. He reminded them that God worked with people like Abraham, Jacob, and Joseph long before the temple and the law came to be. He talked to them about how Israelites in the past refused to be led by God's messengers. He warned them not to be like those Israelites who refused to listen, but to instead listen to God's greatest prophet— Jesus. Stephen called him "the Righteous One" (v. 52). Sadly, in the end, Stephen's accusers chose to keep their old ways and not accept Jesus as their Savior.

Stephen was tragically murdered, making him the first Christian martyr. He died for his faith, and he did so with incredible grace and compassion for his attackers. His final words—"Lord, do not hold this sin against them" (v. 60)—showed that he understood his physical death paled in comparison to being eternally separate from God.

delight |

Stop and consider what Jesus did by dying on the cross for your sins. How does His sacrifice impact you today?

How do you think God speaks to people today? Is it similar or different from Bible days? Why?

display |

Knowing Jesus is life-changing. Without Jesus, we would all be separated from God because of our sin. His death and resurrection changes all of that for us. Because of Him, we have hope that death is not the end for us. He conquered death. Don't be like the Israelites who refused to listen, but take the study of His Word seriously. Devote yourself to completing this book and to go on and study more and more. It's worth your time and attention to build your own personal relationship with Jesus.

Think through the following to help you dive back in to studying God's Word after you complete this devotional. Highlight or circle any of the options that you think will be helpful to you.

I'll keep studying by ...

◆ Reading a specific book of the Bible (Book Name: _____)
◆ Choosing another devotional book (Name: _____)
◆ Creating a prayer journal
◆ Taking notes on what I read
◆ Gathering other godly girls to study with me
◆ Setting aside time to study each day
◆ Memorizing Scripture regularly
◆ Meeting with a mentor, a godly woman who's mature in her faith, to discuss what I'm learning
◆ Joining a small group at my church if I haven't already
◆ Teaching someone younger or new to the faith about what I'm learning

---

Maybe you have never trusted Jesus to lead you in life. Maybe you haven't been listening to Him much at all. Talk to Him about your relationship with Him. Ask Him to begin working on your heart in order to motivate you to listen to Him more. Then, thank Jesus that because of His death and resurrection, you are not separated from God.

The Message Spreads

discover |

READ ACTS 8.

When Philip ran up to it, he heard him reading the prophet Isaiah, and said, "Do you understand what you're reading?"
"How can I," he said, "unless someone guides me?" So he invited Philip to come up and sit with him. —Acts 8:30–31

Have you ever felt confused when reading your Bible? Are there times when you feel like it's written in a foreign language? There are people, customs, and cultures written about that you have no connection to. There are metaphors and images that seem odd and out of place. How are you to understand it all? These thoughts and questions were common among Gentiles (people who are not Jewish) who started reading the Scriptures for the first time. Gentiles didn't grow up hearing the stories about a future promised Savior. They didn't know about God's plan from creation. They would need some help learning the significance of Jesus and why He was such a big deal.

It is important to realize that God had knowledge of the Ethiopian man before Philip met him on the road from Jerusalem. God knew the Ethiopian went to Jerusalem to worship Him. He knew the Ethiopian read the Scriptures, but couldn't make any sense out of it. He saw all of this man's work to get to know Him better. God saw, and God did not leave him alone to figure it out by himself. God sent Philip to guide him.

Philip couldn't have asked for a more willing person to hear about Jesus. He found the man reading the Old Testament! Yet the Ethiopian needed help to understand what he was reading. The Bible is a wonderful tool, and without it, we would be lost in our faith. But we also need teachers. We need both the Bible and the guidance of people further along in their faith to help us grow in our understanding of God.

delight |

Name one girl or woman who has helped you understand the Bible better. What difference did it make for you?

How does knowing God sees all the small efforts you make to learn about Him change your attitude toward reading the Bible on your own?

display |

God notices when you are searching for Him. Just like the Ethiopian, He sees your efforts to get to know Him better. Don't give up on reading the Bible even when it's confusing. Your efforts are not useless. Start making a list of questions you have as you read the Bible. Begin asking your questions to Bible teachers God has already placed in your life. If you don't have anyone to teach you, find a local church to faithfully attend in order to help you understand the Scriptures.

Thank God that He gave us the Bible in order to know Him better. Thank Him for your local church that provides teaching to help you understand it more clearly. Talk to God about any difficulties you have when you read the Bible and acknowledge that He sees all your efforts. Praise Him for being a God who notices even the smallest of efforts you put forth to know Him.

A Change of Perspective

discover |

READ ACTS 9.

As he traveled and was nearing Damascus, a light from heaven suddenly flashed around him. Falling to the ground, he heard a voice saying to him, "Saul, Saul, why are you persecuting me?" "Who are you, Lord?" Saul said. "I am Jesus, the one you are persecuting," he replied. —Acts 9:3-5

Saul was one of the religious leaders present for and supportive of Stephen's murder (see Acts 7:59; 8:1). Now, he was set on destroying the church. He invaded homes and violently took Christians to prison. Imagine your mom or dad or even yourself being forcefully removed from your home simply because of your beliefs! Saul must've been so overcome with hatred for Christians to do something so awful.

For some reason, Jesus showed mercy on Saul. It may seem irrational what God did—saving Saul instead of striking him dead—but He did. This shows us that God will welcome even the most wicked of people to His family if they will repent and follow Him. When Saul met Jesus, his life was forever changed. He underwent one of the most radical changes of anyone who came to Jesus. Saul went from being a violent opponent of the church to boldly proclaiming Jesus as God.

Understandably, Saul's change of heart was confusing to other Christians. They were very cautious of believing in Saul's conversion. It took some time for them to come around to accepting him, but Saul was persistent. Finally, Saul did make new friends. Building a group of Christian friends was vital for Saul's future and the success of completing God's purpose for his life.

delight |

Can you recall any changes in your life from experiencing Jesus? If so, record them here.

Name a few Christian girls who encourage you. Why are they so important to you?

display |

Change is rarely easy. Saul's road to change began with a voice from heaven, a flash of light, and temporary blindness. Your change will most likely be more subtle. Maybe it starts with a desire for justice or service or simply a desire to know Jesus better. Whatever desire comes over you for good and personal knowledge of Jesus, follow it. As you do, change will come. It may feel awkward at times to follow Jesus's commands, but surrounding yourself with friends who also want to follow Jesus helps tremendously.

Write the name of a girl who's pursuing Jesus but isn't part of your friend group. Consider grabbing coffee with her or inviting her to sit with you at lunch.

Look back at the girls you mentioned earlier who encourage you. Write out one way you can encourage each of them in the next week.

List one way having friendships with these girls has changed you for the better and pushed you closer to Jesus.

Pray for God to give you the desire for change that matures you as a Christ-follower. Ask for friends and mentors that support you in that goal. Also ask that God will change you to be receptive to the desires He brings in your heart.

DAY 10

A Message for All

discover |

READ ACTS 10.

A voice said to him, "Get up, Peter; kill and eat." "No Lord!" Peter said. "For I have never eaten anything impure and ritually unclean." Again, a second time, the voice said to him, "What God has made clean, do not call impure." —Acts 10:13-15

Cornelius was a centurion, which meant he was a Roman soldier. He was not a Jew, but he obviously wanted to know the God the Jews worshiped. He did his best to be friendly with the Jews, but he was not included in their group. He was excluded from their religious holidays. He was not allowed in the temple at Jerusalem. He feared God and prayed to Him, but there were definite markers that Cornelius was an outsider in his own belief system.

Peter received a vision. In the vision, God told him that animals once thought "unclean" by Jewish God-given law were now declared clean. Peter was confused. Why would God want him to disregard the law? It all became clear to Peter when he met with Cornelius. It was no coincidence that Peter was called to see Cornelius at the same time he was thinking over this vision. Peter said: "it's forbidden for a Jewish man to associate with or visit a foreigner, but God has shown me that I must not call any person impure" (v. 28). The vision was a lesson to Peter about people who weren't Jews being accepted into God's family of believers. Jesus's message was a message for all.

This moment in history was monumental for all Christians going forward. There was so much focus at that time on what people did or didn't do, what they ate or didn't eat, where they worshiped or didn't worship. At this moment, God declared, "No more!" What God says is good is good, and God showed that Cornelius was clean by granting him the Holy Spirit.

Presence and Purpose

delight |

Is there something or someone you have decided is "bad" but need to reconsider based on today's lesson? Who or what?

As Christians, what is our measuring stick for what is good or not?

display |

Be careful about what lines or boundaries you draw around your faith. Always check God's Word and think through what is essential and what is not. Remember what makes someone a Christian is God's presence living in that person. It's not based on a list of dos and don'ts. Think about the things you do that are related to your faith. Make sure you do not consider those things as what makes you a Christian.

Thank God that He doesn't exclude anyone from Jesus. Pray that you will be a good ambassador of Christ to others and ask God to bring people into your life whom you can extend goodwill to. If there is a girl you have a difficult time relating to, ask God to help you connect with her so that Jesus may be glorified.

THE MISSIONARY MOVEMENT

The Holy Spirit had come and the message of Jesus was spreading like wildfire in Jerusalem. However, opponents of Jesus were becoming more and more infuriated. At this stage, the story took an ugly turn. The resistance became more violent (see Acts 11). Followers of Jesus were forced to flee Jerusalem for their lives, but as they went, they didn't lose their faith. They took the message of Jesus to those outside Jerusalem, and it spread exponentially. What was once a movement focused in Jerusalem was on its way to being a worldwide phenomenon. This part of the book of Acts also shifts focus from the first disciples and centers on a man named Saul, whose devotion to the message of Jesus would not only change the early church, but would also change Christianity for generations to come—including ours.

You've Got a Friend

discover |

READ ACTS 11.

Then he went to Tarsus to search for Saul, and when he found him he brought him to Antioch. For a whole year they met with the church and taught large numbers. The disciples were first called Christians at Antioch. —*Acts 11:25–26*

The Gentile church was booming. After Philip's trip to Samaria, Peter's experience with Cornelius, and now large numbers of Greek believers in Antioch, there was no denying the growth of non-Jewish believers. This Gentile church was growing so fast that news had spread all the way to Jerusalem. The apostles chose Barnabas to go to Antioch to find out whether all these new believers were legit.

Barnabas was sent to find out answers to questions such as "Are they worshiping Jesus?" and "Is the Spirit present?" Barnabas found that this church was filled with God's presence and the people were devoted to Jesus. Seeing God's presence among the Gentiles was an undeniable indicator that God was welcoming all kinds of people into His family, not just Jews.

Then Barnabas went out to bring Saul to Antioch. Barnabas trusted Saul. He wanted Saul to be a part of this growing church and to teach them. Don't miss this—Barnabas chose a former persecutor of Christians to lead! Barnabas must've been the type of person who believed in people despite their past. His confidence in Saul put him in a place of authority and leadership for the new church. By giving Saul this chance, Barnabas set Saul up to make an enormous impact on the early church that resonates even today.

delight |

What actions or words from others make you feel that people have confidence in you?

Who is a girl who needs your confidence? Is there a girl you know who is new in the faith that needs encouragement? Write her name here.

display |

It can be difficult to show confidence in someone who has a bad history, but God is able to work in even the most tarnished of people. It can make a world of difference to a person when someone believes in them. Your confidence in another person can have effects not only on their circle of influence, but in the generations to come.

Think of a girl who could use your trust in her today. Notice the words you speak and the actions you take. Do they convey confidence in her? If not, how can you change them? If so, what other encouraging words and actions come to mind?

Thank God for the girls in your life who encourage you. If you don't have a girl in your life like that, then pray for one to come into your life who will. Ask God to show you the girls around you who need encouragement and ask for His Spirit to give you the words and actions that will encourage them.

God Only Knows

discover |

READ ACTS 12.

Suddenly an angel of the Lord appeared, and a light shone in the cell. Striking Peter on the side, he woke him up and said, "Quick, get up!" And the chains fell off his wrists. —Acts 12:7

Things were getting tough for Jesus's disciples. James, one of the original twelve disciples, was executed. He was one of Jesus's closest friends. Then Peter was arrested, and he was probably expecting the same outcome James received. For some reason, Peter's story didn't end there. Peter's escape sounds like something out of a fairy tale: an angel appeared to Peter and led him out of the jail. His chains just fell off. Then they walked past multiple guards unnoticed. The city gates miraculously opened for them like they were entering a store.

But Peter's escape was not the only unbelievable event in this chapter. King Herod suddenly fell over dead because he didn't give glory to God. He allowed people to worship him instead of the real God, and for that, God struck him dead. God's power is beyond any jail cell man can create, and it is strong enough to eliminate any bully or tyrant.

You may be thinking: I wish God acted like this every day—freeing the innocent and punishing the wicked. The reality is that sometimes He doesn't. Some days, the wicked win and the innocent get hurt. But we must realize that some days, we are the ones who have done wrong, and we are glad He doesn't punish us in that moment. He gives us a chance to try again and make amends. From Acts 12, we can learn that when He does choose to intervene, He always does what is right.

delight |

In what ways have you seen God working circumstances for those in need and/or against the proud?

Why do you think God sometimes waits to rescue the innocent and punish the proud?

display |

It can be difficult to accept God's plans when we see the wicked win and the innocent get punished. These are circumstances that are beyond our understanding. No one knows why God chooses to intervene at some moments and not at others, but we can rest assured of His goodness and His presence. He promises to be near the broken-hearted (see Ps. 34:18) and oppose the proud (see 1 Pet 5:5). Just never stop communicating with Him when things are tough. He'll show you the way. In the space provided, write out a declaration of your trust in Him, regardless of how situations seem.

Take time to acknowledge God's presence even in difficult circumstances. Thank Him for being with you always. Praise Him that He will one day make all wrongs right. Pray for understanding when circumstances don't make sense. Ask Him to teach you to be faithful when you feel neglected.

For a Specific Purpose

discover |

READ ACTS 13.

As they were worshiping the Lord and fasting, the Holy Spirit said, "Set apart for me Barnabas and Saul for the work to which I have called them." Then after they had fasted, prayed, and laid hands on them, they sent them off. —Acts 13:2-3

After catching his audience up on Peter in Acts 12, Luke (the author of Acts) turned the story back to Saul. At one very special worship service in Antioch, the Holy Spirit spoke, asking Saul (who became known as Paul in this chapter) and Barnabas to be set apart for a special work. It is unclear how the Spirit was heard, but it was obviously accepted by all present that Paul and Barnabas had been given a specific purpose to go out from the church and the church was to support them.

Here, we see the church purposely sending out members for the goal of spreading the good news of Jesus. Instead of persecution stopping the spread of the gospel, the church took an active and intentional step to get the word of Jesus out to those who didn't know Him. For those reasons, Barnabas and Paul are considered the first missionaries.

When Paul and Barnabas visited a city, they would first go to the Jewish people. They were both of Jewish heritage, so a synagogue would be a great location to meet with others interested in the workings of God. They clearly presented Jesus as the fulfillment of all the Jewish prophecies. Many believed, but others resisted. The opposition these men experienced in Cyprus and Pisidia was only the beginning, but these men were relentless in their mission. They were certain of their calling, certain of their message, and certain of their life's purpose.

delight |

Are you certain of Jesus's purpose for you? Why or why not?

What role does the local church play in you living out your purpose in life?

display |

For most of us, God doesn't speak to a whole church about what our specific purpose in life will be, but He does provide general guidelines. There are so many instructions in the Bible of what we are to do for "one another"—love one another (see John 13:34), encourage one another (see 1 Thess. 5:11), serve one another (see Gal. 5:13), and so on. The best place to begin doing these things is in the local church. Begin dreaming, planning, and brainstorming ways you can be more active in your church. As you practice the general "one another" commands, you'll find you are living out God's specific purpose for your life. List three ways you can be more involved in your local church.

1.

2.

3.

> **Talk to God about your local church. Name the things you are thankful for about your church. Tell Him about the things you'd like to see your church doing that maybe it isn't able to do right now. Ask God to show you opportunities to help others in your church. Thank Him for any encouragement you receive from fellow believers. Pray that He will show the way to living out His specific purpose for your life.**

The First Missionary Journey

discover |

READ ACTS 14.

After they arrived and gathered the church together, they reported everything God had done with them and that he had opened the door of faith to the Gentiles. —Acts 14:27

Barnabas and Paul continued their mission to share Jesus with as many people as possible. Their message in Iconium attracted a crowd of Jews and Gentiles. There were those who didn't believe them, so they started spreading rumors about Paul and Barnabas. Paul and Barnabas, however, didn't let the rumors get to them. They were persistent and didn't fold to the viciousness of others.

In Lystra, Paul healed a lame man through the power of the Spirit. In response to the miracle they just witnessed, the people of Lystra believed Paul and Barnabas were Greek gods. They wanted to worship them. Paul and Barnabas who were almost stoned to death a few days prior were now being worshiped! They, however, knew better than to fall into the temptation of letting other people worship them. They were wiser than to let that happen.

Things turned bad in Lystra when Jews from neighboring towns came and began spreading rumors again. They turned the crowds against Paul and Barnabas. Paul was nearly stoned to death! Praise God, Paul had friends to come to his aid. Despite the toxicity of their opposition, many people did come to faith. Churches were established and people were changed for the better. Finally, Paul and Barnabas made their way back to their home church in Antioch where they were certainly relieved to see friendly faces and an established church. Whether among friends or foes, Paul and Barnabas preached Jesus continually.

delight |

How do you respond when someone has a negative opinion about you?

What are the dangers of being praised by others?

display |

Whether we like to admit it or not, others' opinions about us can have a big impact on our outlook on life. It is good to have a group of friends like Paul and Barnabas had in Antioch to come back to and know you are welcomed just as you are; but there will be moments when you aren't welcomed. In these moments, you need to be certain of God's purpose for you. Ask yourself these questions when you find people's opinions starting to get to you: "Who do I belong to?" "Who am I really serving at this moment?" "Is it God or myself?"

Thank God for loving you so much that He sent Jesus to you. Read Romans 8:31-39 if you need some reassurance. Ask God to make you confident in His love for you. Pray that you will be assured of your purpose to share Jesus even when people have a negative opinion about you.

Much Debate

discover |

READ ACTS 15.

"And God, who knows the heart, bore witness to them by giving them the Holy Spirit, just as he also did to us. He made no distinction between us and them, cleansing their hearts by faith." —Acts 15:8-9

The debate held at the Jerusalem Council was a monumental decision about how Christianity was to be lived out in individual lives. Here was the basic question being debated: were Gentiles required to keep the Old Testament law? Remember, the message of Jesus was given first to the Jews. Now the Jews were split about what from God's instructions to them in the past were required of all Christians.

The Bible says there was "much debate" (v. 7), meaning the final decision didn't come easily. Just because everyone in the room trusted in Jesus and had the Holy Spirit didn't mean they would all agree on how to live out the details of the Christian life. In the end, though, an agreement was made. They decided that if God had chosen to give the Gentiles the Holy Spirit, including them in His chosen people, then the apostles shouldn't add an extra burden on them. They acknowledged that they were saved by the grace of Jesus and so were the Gentiles. No one—not the Jews and not the Gentiles—was saved by keeping laws.

The final decision was that Gentiles were not required to keep the law and be circumcised. There were a few restrictions the apostles gave to the Gentiles, but these restrictions were not necessary for salvation. These restrictions were for protecting the new believers from falling into temptation and tarnishing their witness to unbelievers.

delight |

What would you say to a girl who asked you what makes someone a Christian?

What are some wise decisions you could make that don't define you as a Christian, but are good decisions in light of today's culture?

display |

You are saved by the grace of Jesus through faith and not by a set of laws that you have to keep (see Eph. 2:8-9). Let that truth settle in your heart. Don't judge yourself or others by some standard of Christianity that God never intended for you. Do, however, take the time to examine your behaviors.

Is there something you personally should avoid? Jot it down and practice avoiding that thing.

Do you notice a change when you eliminate it? It may be a sign you need to make some personal restrictions for yourself or avoid it all together.

Thank God for the grace of Jesus given to you that you are welcomed into His family just as you are. Relish the generosity of God's goodness to you: you are not required to keep a set of laws to be in relationship with Him. Then ask Him to help you make wise decisions to keep you from falling into sin and to make you a faithful witness.

Hope, Confidence, Devotion

discover |

READ ACTS 16.

About midnight Paul and Silas were praying and singing hymns to God, and the prisoners were listening to them. Suddenly there was such a violent earthquake that the foundations of the jail were shaken, and immediately all the doors were opened, and everyone's chains came loose. —Acts 16:25–26

While on this second missionary journey, Paul encountered a slave girl possessed by an evil spirit. This evil spirit gave the girl the ability to tell the future. It made her owners very wealthy as they exploited her abilities for their own gain. So, it was very upsetting to the owners when Paul "fixed" her by casting out the evil spirit. They weren't interested in seeing this girl well or happy or finally free. They were only interested in what they could get out of her for themselves.

Paul and Silas found themselves imprisoned for their "good deed." Their response to imprisonment is an inspiration for any of us today who find ourselves in a miserable situation. They prayed and sang hymns to God while sitting in a jail cell! These men did not lose their hope, their confidence, or their devotion to God even when things looked bad.

Amazingly, God intervened by sending an earthquake that broke all the prisoners' chains. Everyone was free to walk out of their jail cell and go home. The jailer was about to kill himself because if his boss came down in the morning and saw no prisoners, he would've been executed. Not only that, but his family would've been disgraced. By killing himself, he would've spared his family shame. Paul stopped this suicide attempt by letting the guard know no one had escaped. Paul shows us in this chapter that people are not to be used for our selfish gain. People are valuable in the sight of God and worthy of our service and kindness.

delight |

What might be a situation where you need to lay aside your rights for the sake of someone else?

Have you ever had a situation where something terrible turned for good? How did you see God move in that situation?

display |

God makes it clear that He cares for people. He wants His people to care for others as well. In Matthew 25, Jesus said whatever we do to help the least among us is directly serving Him. He identifies with those who need help, and He wants His people to be His hands and feet to help them. Sometimes it will require laying aside our own agenda. God's purpose must take priority if we are to call ourselves His people.

Name a girl who could use your kindness today. How will you show her kindness?

Talk to God about the times you have a hard time being kind. Tell Him about the girls in your life you'd like to show kindness but struggle to follow through. Ask Him to show you girls who need your help and ask Him to give you the strength to serve them.

MEMORY VERSE

Acts 16:25-26

ABOUT MIDNIGHT PAUL AND SILAS WERE PRAYING AND SINGING HYMNS TO GOD, AND THE PRISONERS WERE LISTENING TO THEM. SUDDENLY THERE WAS SUCH A VIOLENT EARTHQUAKE THAT THE FOUNDATIONS OF THE JAIL WERE SHAKEN, AND IMMEDIATELY ALL THE DOORS WERE OPENED, AND EVERYONE'S CHAINS CAME LOOSE.

DAY 17

A Different Approach

discover |

READ ACTS 17.

"For as I was passing through and observing the objects of your worship, I even found an altar on which was inscribed: 'To an Unknown God.' Therefore, what you worship in ignorance, this I proclaim to you." —Acts 17:23

When Paul came to a new town, he would usually visit the local synagogue first. While in the synagogue, Paul understood that the people listening would be concerned about learning and understanding the Old Testament Scriptures. They would understand the problem of sin and the need to be restored in a right relationship with God. So when he addressed them, he would talk about how Jesus fits all of the Old Testament prophecies for the long-awaited Savior (or Messiah). He did his best to show how Jesus was the answer to their searching.

When Paul arrived in Athens, he was deeply distressed at how many idols he saw there. He knew he would need a different approach with these people. The people of Athens weren't concerned with Old Testament prophecies. They were concerned with how the universe worked. Who made the earth and all the creatures in it? Who made man and thought through everything he would need to survive? What divine beings might exist that we can't see?

When Paul spoke about Jesus to others, he addressed their situation. He observed and studied his audience. When we read Acts, it can feel like it's a succession of quick events, but Paul took his time in these cities. Sometimes he'd spend months or even years in a location. He valued people's thoughtful questions and engaged them with the answers he had learned from studying the Scriptures for himself.

delight |

What are some questions you or your friends struggle to find the answers to?

How can God help you answer these questions?

display |

Think about the questions you have in your heart—questions that stir your desire for study, that change the way you view the world around you, and that affect your everyday decisions. Journal your questions. Talk them over with God and other trusted friends and mentors. The more of these types of questions you can answer for yourself, the more you can help others find answers as well. Next, begin listening to others—genuinely listen to them. Ask them questions to help you better understand what they need help with. Don't assume a one-time conversation will fix all of their problems. Be ready to spend time with others as they work through their own deep questions.

Talk to God about the answers that you search for within your own heart. Ask Him to show you more about Himself as you search for answers. Pray for the girls around you who you know need to be seeking Jesus. Ask God to give you words to speak that will bring them hope and peace.

DAY 18

A Shared Purpose

discover |

READ ACTS 18.

The Lord said to Paul in a night vision, "Don't be afraid, but keep on speaking and don't be silent. For I am with you, and no one will lay a hand on you to hurt you, because I have many people in this city." —Acts 18:9-10

The work Paul was doing was dangerous. There were many people who opposed him, and some even wanted him dead. There were probably times when he felt discouraged and maybe even wanted to quit because of the opposition he faced. It was good that he had people like Aquila, Priscilla, and Apollos to come alongside him and share in his work and ministry. But even better than having people with you is knowing God has your back.

Moments like what we see in the Scripture for today had to feel like a refreshing drink of water after wandering in a dry and dusty desert for Paul. For God to tell him, "Don't be afraid . . . keep on speaking . . . I am with you" (vv. 9-10) must have been empowering, encouraging, and inspiring.

While our mission of making disciples is the same purpose Paul had, most of us have never been faced with life-threatening situations like he faced. However, God offers us the same encouragement and the same presence. He tells us to keep speaking the truth of the gospel to those we come in contact with. He tells us He is with us, and because of this, we can face any challenge we encounter without fear and with confidence. Having friends to walk the journey with us is nice as well. God provides His presence and the presence of others as we follow His purpose for our lives.

Presence and Purpose

delight |

Who are people in your life like Aquila, Priscilla, and Apollos who have a shared purpose like you?

When have you felt encouragement from God to keep going and not be afraid in spite of difficult circumstances?

display |

Even if the opposition we face is not as scary as Paul's was, we still face opposition and can get discouraged at times. In those moments, remember God is with us. His presence fuels our purpose. In the space provided, use the prayer prompt to write out a prayer to God for continued encouragement as you walk the path of purpose He has placed you on.

Thank God for His presence and for the purpose He has given you. Thank Him for the friends He has placed around you who have the same purpose in life. If you do not have friends who share your purpose, ask God to gather girls around you who will walk this journey alongside you.

DAY 19

God Is Not Made

discover |

READ ACTS 19.

"You see and hear that not only in Ephesus, but in almost all of Asia, this man Paul has persuaded and misled a considerable number of people by saying that gods made by hand are not gods." —Acts 19:26

People all over the region who chose to follow the teachings of Jesus were making drastic changes. In Ephesus, numerous people stopped buying idols of the goddess Athena—so many that the craftsmen who made the idols were losing income. These craftsmen grew furious and were determined to put a stop to all this "Jesus talk."

The craftsmen got together and started a commotion for the people to take action against the Christians. They dragged two of Paul's closest friends into an amphitheater, which was the ideal place to draw an even bigger crowd of onlookers. The scene became so chaotic that many in the audience didn't know what they were watching happen. These people were carried away by their desire to see some action and didn't care about who was being harmed. The scene was probably similar to a schoolyard fight.

Luckily, the city clerk broke the whole thing up. Paul's friends evaded a violent mob attack, but the craftsmen of Ephesus made it clear that they wanted no part of Jesus—especially if Jesus cost them their incomes. Their love of money surpassed their desire for truth and human kindness. Loving the revenue of their trade kept them from encountering the riches of Jesus's grace, love, and peace.

delight |

What changes do you think are difficult for someone who wants to follow Jesus?

What are some signs in your life that you are loving something other than Jesus?

display |

An idol is anything we put in a place of worship that is not God. It doesn't have to be a wooden statue. It can be a person, an object, or a position. Here is a helpful gauge on how to determine if something has become an idol for you: If you're willing to sin to get it or if you sin when you don't get it, then the thing you are wanting has become an idol. Watch your actions. If you have gone so far as to sin in such a way that you are treating others cruelly, then you need to stop and examine what it is you are wanting in that moment that you are not getting.

As you go throughout the week, examine your heart. List anything (or anyone) you believe has become an idol to you. Ask God to show you how to set aside those idols and focus your heart on Him.

Ask God to show you any idols you may be holding on to. Seek His help in overcoming them. It is not simply a matter of willpower when it comes to defeating idols. You will need the Spirit's help. Thank Him that there is no enemy He can not defeat.

Passionate About His Purpose

discover |

READ ACTS 20.

"But I consider my life of no value to myself: my purpose is to finish my course and the ministry I received from the Lord Jesus, to testify to the gospel of God's grace." —Acts 20:24

This speech contains Paul's last words to his good friends, the elders of the church in Ephesus. He knew his life was in danger, and although God had spared him numerous times from death, he accepted that it would not always be so (see v. 23). These are the words he wanted his friends to remember him by.

It is clear from Paul's words he wanted his legacy to be about how committed he was to getting the news about Jesus out to as many people as possible. His devotion to his purpose was so fierce that he was ready to give his life up for it. That kind of dedication can change lives, but only if one stays committed to God's plan. Notice that Paul warned the elders about what could get in the way of their devotion. He warned them of false teachers who spread lies only to gain followers (see v. 30). He warned the elders to be on guard against such people not only for their flock, but for themselves (see v. 28).

Abandoning the truth in exchange for followers will wreak havoc on completing God's purpose for your life. Paul recognized it. Paul worked hard and didn't become consumed with how many followers he had. He didn't play the comparison game, but stayed his course (see v. 33). His purpose was so entrenched in his mind that nothing was going to distract him from completing it.

delight |

How do you see girls trade in God's truth and kindness for more followers today?

Which would you choose: a risky life completing God's purpose or a safe life ignoring God's purpose? Why or why not?

display |

Where are your priorities in life? Maybe you're not at the point in your life to say "I'm ready to die for the spread of the gospel," but how about sacrificing a few moments to be a good friend to someone who needs one or sacrificing some personal rights to show someone the love of Christ? Prioritize exhibiting Jesus to others through your words and actions and you are well on your way to completing the purpose God has for you.

Ask the Holy Spirit to guide you as you examine your heart. What are your top five priorities? As you list them, pay attention to what God might be calling you to change or shift to spread the gospel. Then, commit to doing those things.

> **Thank God that someone thought you were important enough to share Jesus with you. Ask God to help you value others enough to share Jesus with them. Admit the times you did not value others and the spread of the gospel enough. Pray that your level of sacrifice will increase over time.**

Presence and Purpose

THE ROAD TO ROME

Paul had undergone an amazing transformation. In the last ten days of this devotional, you will read just how dedicated Paul was to living out the purpose God had for him. He knew his life was in danger, but he considered the call of God on his life to be far more valuable. He also knew that if people did not hear about Jesus, they would die eternally separated from a God who loves them and wants them to be in His family. He was committed to God and committed to everyone everywhere knowing the love of Jesus for themselves.

Faith Over Fear

discover |

READ ACTS 21.

Then Paul replied, "What are you doing, weeping and breaking
my heart? For I am ready not only to be bound but also to die in
Jerusalem for the name of the Lord Jesus." —Acts 21:13

Paul had it on good authority from the Holy Spirit that when he went to Jerusalem, his life would be at risk (see Acts 20:22-23). He was ready to take that chance. He was ready to be bound and executed in order to obey the purpose God had given him. Over and over, Paul's friends pleaded with him not to go to Jerusalem. Understandably, they wanted to spare Paul from this danger. But Paul didn't make decisions based on fear. Paul made his decisions based on God's will for his life.

Paul's heart was breaking over rejecting his friends' advice. Paul wasn't the kind of person who acted superior to his friends when he felt called by God. He didn't talk down to them as though they just "didn't get it." He sympathized with his friends. He felt their pain and truly wanted to ease their anguish, but to obey God was far more valuable to Paul than making his friends happy.

Paul understood the consequences of his choices. He understood that following God's call on his life wouldn't guarantee his safety, but he also understood that the alternative was far worse. Disobeying God wasn't a path Paul wasn't willing to go down. When we understand what we gain when we choose God's way over our own, what seems like a difficult decision becomes much easier.

delight |

What are some fears you have that may be keeping you from stepping out in faith?

Why do you think it is so hard to follow the voice of God above the voice of your friends?

display |

We all have fears that keep us from following God's lead. Name those fears. Discuss them with God. Then spend some time considering what you gain when you trust God. Look up Scriptures about the rewards God gives to those who follow Him. Here are a few verses to look up to get you started: John 15:5-11; Romans 10:11; Ephesians 1:18-19. God has promised you that you won't regret putting your trust in Him (see Rom. 10:11).

Ask God for wisdom in your decision-making. Tell Him about the times you made choices out of fear or to please others. Talk to Him about the kind of decisions you want to make moving forward. If a decision seems difficult, ask for His Spirit to guide you.

Excluding Others

discover |

READ ACTS 22.

They listened to him up to this point. Then they raised their voices, shouting, "Wipe this man off the face of the earth! He should not be allowed to live!" —Acts 22:22

In this chapter of Acts, Paul encountered the trouble he had been warned about by his friends. It all started when he entered the synagogue—in a respectful manner, mind you (see Acts 21:26). The Jews who opposed Paul saw him and knew he was an outspoken teacher of Jesus. They claimed he was against the Jewish people, the law, and the temple (see Acts 21:28). Then they made this statement, which shows the racism they had in their hearts: "[Paul] also brought Greeks into the temple and has defiled this holy place." These men couldn't stand having someone outside their group receiving God's grace.

Things got violent after the men started hurling accusations at Paul. A mob was formed, and they tried to kill Paul! Some Roman soldiers saw the commotion and took Paul into custody. Paul asked the commanding soldier if he could address the crowd. Since the commander couldn't understand what Paul was accused of, he probably hoped Paul's speech would calm down the mob. It did calm the crowd for awhile, until Paul said: "[God] said to me, 'Go, because I will send you far away to the Gentiles'" (v. 21).

The mob yelled back, "Wipe this man off the face of the earth!" (v. 22). These Jews took major issue with including anyone outside their group. Their love for exclusive blessings had overridden their kindness to others, their willingness to listen to others' points of view, and their obedience to God.

delight |

Have you ever experienced being left out because of your race or how you look? How did it make you feel?

Why is it important to not exclude others from hearing about Jesus?

display |

The choice is always present to extend friendship to those outside your circle. If you have ever felt the sting of being left out, you know how important it is for someone to feel welcomed. Think about your groups of friends. Is there a girl who doesn't have many friends that you could invite into one of your friend groups? The difference you make in another girl's life when you include them in your circle can't be stated strongly enough. It might just make an eternal difference for her.

Draw a small circle below and write "Me" in the center. Then draw a slightly bigger circle around that and write the names of your closest friends in it. Then think about the girls you might invite to hang out with you guys and create a small circle for each of their names. As you pray for each girl in the outer circles, draw a line from her name to your inner circle. Let this serve as a reminder to be known for inviting others in rather than excluding them.

> **Thank God that He loves you so much He included you in His family. Tell Him about your own struggles to feel like you fit in a group. Ask Him to show you girls who need to feel included and to give you the confidence to engage them in conversation.**

DAY 23
Have Courage

discover |

READ ACTS 23.

The following night, the Lord stood by him and said, "Have courage! For as you have testified about me in Jerusalem, so it is necessary for you to testify in Rome." —Acts 23:11

Have you ever wondered if what you were doing was wrong because you weren't seeing the results you wanted? Maybe you've studied for a test and you still failed, or maybe you practiced really hard but you don't see a difference in your performance, or maybe you've shared Jesus with someone and they still think you're crazy. It can be difficult to keep moving forward when circumstances don't seem to change. Paul had a moment like that in Jerusalem. He spoke to Jews all over the region, and time after time, they rejected his message and even wanted him dead.

God stepped in at a time when Paul needed courage to persevere. God knew of Paul's faithfulness in the past and He called Paul to be faithful going forward. That's what doing the right thing feels like sometimes: continuing to be faithful even when the results aren't what we want them to be. When we choose to follow God, we leave the results up to Him. We don't abandon our purpose when the road gets rocky. We remain faithful to our calling and trust that even if things aren't going how we thought they would, God is still in control.

When you abandon faithfulness to God, you are leaving the results of your life up to someone else who is not all-powerful, all-knowing, and supremely good. You can't change hearts or minds like God can. You can't change the weather or world rulers or future events. It is much better to remain faithful and trust God to handle the outcome because He is capable of the job.

delight |

What's your reaction when the results are not what you have worked so hard to achieve? How can God's words to Paul apply to you?

How might your attitude be different if you trusted God for the results and just remained faithful?

display |

It can be extremely frustrating when you try to be faithful and life keeps handing you disappointments. Consider the alternative: if life only handed you success, would you ever seek out God? It's those tough times that show us our need for God. It's those times that show us we are not in control of the world. Abandoning God's purpose should not be an option for you. He is the only one who can work all things together for good (see Rom. 8:28). Trust Him.

In the space below, write out a declaration of your trust in Him. It can be a prayer, a poem, or just the first thoughts that come to your head. Just tell Him how you feel. He understands and wants to hear your heart.

> **Think about your latest disappointment that was not due to anything you did wrong. Lean into God. Take some deep breaths to calm your inner dialogue about how horrible life is and just hold out open hands to God. Release your disappointments to Him. Cry to Him if necessary. He sees, He knows, and He loves you more than you know.**

Building Connections

discover |

READ ACTS 24.

"But I admit this to you: I worship the God of my ancestors according to the Way, which they call a sect, believing everything that is in accordance with the law and written in the prophets." —Acts 24:14

In Acts 24, Paul was accused of being "an agitator" (v. 5). The prosecutor in Paul's hearing, Tertullus, wanted to make the case that Paul was causing fights and uproars among the people. He was ready to paint the picture of Paul being a menace to society. He even called him "a plague" (v. 5). He figured the governor would surely punish someone who was such a delinquent.

When it was Paul's turn to speak, he explained to Felix, the governor, how he didn't start the fight in Jerusalem. It was the men who started yelling at him while he was in the temple that caused the uproar (see Acts 21:26-30). Paul made it clear he didn't go about arguing with people or causing a disturbance. In other words, his behavior was polite to others and respectful to the community.

Sometimes in our fervor to persuade others, we can get a bit argumentative. We can call people names or raise our voices. It is possible that others may turn disrespectful when you share about Jesus, but that's not the way of Jesus, and it wasn't Paul's approach either. Paul sought to make connections with others. He spoke of how he worshiped the same God the men who accused him claimed to worship. Paul wanted to see people become his brothers and sisters in Christ and he had no intention to make enemies.

delight |

What causes you to lose your cool in a conflict? Do you call people names or raise your voice? How can you model Paul's approach of seeking to make connections next time?

What have been your experiences when talking to people of different faiths? What might you be able to do to keep the conversation moving in a productive direction?

display |

Differences of opinion will come up when you talk to others about their beliefs. It's almost inevitable. Be prepared to handle those disagreements with grace. Remind yourself that the goal is not to be the loudest or the most forceful or even to win the argument. That was the way of Paul's accusers. Follow Paul's approach and Jesus's as well. Seek to serve and understand. Find points of agreement and build relationships.

Think of a girl you know who has different beliefs from you. Write out her name and one point of agreement you have with her. Knowing this ahead of time will help you have those difficult conversations when the time comes.

Maybe you've handled disagreements in the past poorly. Admit your mistakes to God. No one is perfect. Remember that you need help from God's Spirit. Talk to God about how you'd like to handle discussions with others in the future. Ask Him to keep sending people in your life who have different beliefs than you so you can keep practicing sharing Jesus with them in a gracious manner.

Memory Verse
Acts 23:11

The following night, the Lord stood by him and said, "Have courage! For as you have testified about me in Jerusalem, so it is necessary for you to testify in Rome."

DAY 25

Determined to Go to Rome

discover |

READ ACTS 25.

*"If then I did anything wrong and am deserving of death, I am not trying
to escape death: but if there is nothing to what these men accuse me of, no
one can give me up to them. I appeal to Caesar!" —Acts 25:11*

Paul had been put off for two years! He had been left to sit in prison
all because Felix, the governor, didn't want to deal with him. He didn't
believe Paul was guilty of a crime, but he didn't want the Jews to get
upset if he set him free, so he made Paul wait. After Felix came Festus,
and he didn't know what to do with Paul either. He went through
protocol and had Paul stand before his accusers while both sides
presented their cases. In the end, he reacted in much the same way
as Felix. He didn't see a reason to punish Paul, but he didn't want the
Jews getting upset with him either.

Have you ever felt stuck in life based on someone else's indecisiveness?
Maybe a college hasn't responded to your application yet, or maybe
you're waiting on a certain guy to ask you on a date, or maybe you're
waiting on your parents to make a decision about something you
really want to do. You are desperate for an answer, but they just won't
provide one. Imagine Paul having to wait years for his answer. That kind
of waiting can weigh on a person so heavily you begin to lose hope.
You may think God has abandoned you at the moment, but the reality
is, He hasn't. Paul's time came. Festus said Paul would go to Rome.
Paul never lost faith that God would do what He said.

delight |

Do you find Paul's persistence in faith in Jesus inspiring? Why or why not?

What areas are you struggling to remain patient and hopeful while feeling "stuck in life"?

display |

Waiting is hard. We can begin to think God has abandoned us when we are waiting, but He promises His presence at all times. So even if you are waiting, you can keep on talking to Him. Waiting doesn't mean sitting on the sidelines or being lazy. It means building relationships in the waiting. Maybe God has you somewhere for the purpose of helping someone else. Look around your situation and stop thinking, "This stinks." Begin thinking, "What can I do in this time of waiting to benefit my relationship with God and my relationship with the people around me?" Journal any ideas that come to mind.

Tell God about any situation you are in where you feel stuck. It's completely okay to ask God to get you out of it. You are not less of a Christian for admitting you want the waiting to end. Then, ask God to keep you hopeful and faithful to Him while you wait. Pray that your circumstances will never cause you to stop trusting that He is good, He is present, and He is working in your life.

Not the Same

discover |

READ ACTS 26.

"Instead, I preached to those in Damascus first, and to those in Jerusalem and in all the region of Judea, and to the Gentiles, that they should repent and turn to God, and do works worthy of repentance." —Acts 26:20

How is your life different now than it was a year ago? Two years ago? Five years ago? Maybe you live in a new town or go to a different school. Perhaps you have different friends, or you stopped playing one sport and started another, or you joined the band or the choir. You are probably smarter, wiser, and more aware of the world around you. In ways, it can feel like you are a completely different person. However, most of the changes you've undergone over the last few years happened gradually. The change that occurred in Paul's life wasn't gradual, it was abrupt and radical. He didn't just seem different, he really was a completely different person. The changes that had taken place in his heart, his life, and his mission were so drastic that no one could deny what God had done in his life.

Paul had just appealed to Rome, but Festus would have to write to Caesar explaining the situation with Paul. Apparently, Festus didn't really understand it. In Acts 26, Festus asked Agrippa II, the Roman appointed King of Israel, to talk to Paul. Being more acquainted with Jewish law and religion, Festus figured Agrippa was more likely to be able to get to the bottom of the situation. Instead, Paul proceeded to share his story. He shared about his former life as a Pharisee and violent opponent of Christianity who went so far as to see to it that Christians were put to death. Now, we find Paul urging both Agrippa and Festus to put their trust in Jesus. There is no adequate explanation for Paul's radical shift in his life and mission except that he really did meet the resurrected Jesus on the road to Damascus and he really did discover that Jesus is the Messiah. This good news changes everything.

delight |

Look at verses 6-8. Why had Paul been arrested? Why is the resurrection such a big deal?

Why did Paul remind Agrippa and Festus of who he was before coming to faith in Christ? What does this tell you about the power of God in Paul's life?

display |

Paul went from being a violent opponent of Christians to being someone who boldly challenged kings and governors to trust Jesus. Paul's story is not only one of the most powerful stories of transformation in the Bible but also in all of human history. Remember that the same God who rescued and redeemed Paul and gave him a new hope offers to do the same for you. You may not experience transformation that looks anywhere near as dramatic as what Paul experienced, but our God is in the business of transformation, and He wants to transform your hope, focus, purpose, and mission.

Do you think of yourself as someone who is living on mission for Christ? Explain. What is one step you could take to do so?

Ask God to open your eyes to the ways you are in need of transformation. Ask Him to renew your hope, refocus your purpose, and open your eyes to the ways He wants to use you to love and serve others. Ask Him to help you take one step this week toward living more deliberately on mission for Jesus.

DAY 27

Hardships Will Happen

discover |

READ ACTS 27:1-26.

"So take courage, men, because I believe God that it will be just the way it was told to me." —Acts 27:25

Have you ever felt like there was a situation in your life that just kept getting gradually worse and no matter what you tried to do to fix it, things just seemed to never get better? That's more or less what we see the sailors in this passage doing. They are doing all the things that they knew to do from their training as professional sailors and soldiers, yet none of their efforts made the situation any better, and they couldn't figure out why.

Paul, who was being transported to Rome, in contrast to the sailors, did not let this incredibly trying situation move him to despair. Paul seized this anxiety-filled moment to encourage and challenge his captors not to lose hope. He even went so far as to assure them that they would not lose their lives because an angel of the Lord met him in a vision telling Paul that it was necessary for him to appear before Caesar (see vv. 24-25). For Paul, this incredibly difficult situation was an opportunity for ministry and encouragement.

It can be really hard to see the opportunities for ministry and encouragement difficulty often brings, but when people are overwhelmed by their problems and cannot seem to fix them, they are more likely to listen to the hope we have to offer them.

delight |

How can you find courage and hope when nothing seems to be going right? How might such situations actually be opportunities for ministry?

What high-pressure or really difficult situation are you facing right now? How might Paul's example encourage you?

display |

Wouldn't you love it if an angel of the Lord would assure you that everything was going to be okay? God may not speak to you through angels like he did for Paul, but He does speak to you constantly. The clearest way God speaks is through His Word. This story you just read, if you will listen, offers you hope and perspective on the greatest sources of anxiety in your life. This story reminds us that God is in control and He protects, guides, and sustains His people as they live on mission for Him. You may not know what the future holds, but you can live with the confidence that God is with you and for you.

Write out some truths you've "heard" as you've studied God's Word this week.

Thank God for His promise to be with you, to protect you, and to sustain you. Ask Him to help you remember that He is always with you and wants to empower you and strengthen you as you live on mission for Him. His presence fuels your purpose.

DAY 28

No One Harmed

discover |

READ ACTS 27:27-28:10.

"So I urge you to take some food. For this is for your survival, since none of you will lose a hair from your head." —Acts 27:34

Most people love stories of dramatic reversals—like stories where the goofy guy gets the girl, or the terrible football team somehow wins the state title, or where an old, run-down house is turned into a beautiful home. The Bible is full of such stories. As we have seen, Paul's Damascus road experience was one of the most dramatic reversals in human history. Here, however, we see another story along similar lines. Paul essentially transitions from a lowly prisoner being transported by centurions to Rome to being the unofficial leader of the ship he was on in the middle of a shipwreck.

In this passage, we see God use Paul's leadership, faith, and love to save lives. In fact, it was thanks to Paul's relationship with the centurion that the lives of the prisoners on the boat were saved. This story reminds us that God is constantly at work even when we might not recognize it. It is also a story that reminds us of the power of relationships. Had Paul not shown love to and built a relationship with the centurion, he and the other prisoners would have lost their lives. God, however, had more ministry in mind for Paul. He has more ministry in mind for you as well. Use Paul's example as fuel to step into that ministry with confidence in God and hope for the future.

delight |

How did Paul's words and example impact the centurion? What can you learn from his example?

What is a story from your own life where God offered hope in a seemingly hopeless situation?

display |

Once again, this passage reminds us that seemingly hopeless situations can be really great opportunities for ministry. When things are rough in the lives of the people around you, they are more likely to be open to hearing about the hope you have in Christ. However, always remember that relationships matter. Don't treat people like projects. Love them and serve them as you seek to share your hope in Christ with them.

What is one way you could offer hope or encouragement to a girl in your life this week?

Ask God to help you identify the ministry He is calling you to. Ask Him to help you embrace this ministry with confidence in Him and hope for the future.

The Sweetness of Friendship

discover |

READ ACTS 28:11-29.

Now the brothers and sisters from there had heard the news about us and had come to meet us as far as the Forum of Appius and the Three Taverns. When Paul saw them, he thanked God and took courage. —Acts 28:15

Have you ever dreaded having to do something you knew would turn out bad? Maybe you had to confront someone about an issue you have with them or you had to confess to your parents about something you did wrong. Paul knew that, once again, he had to speak to a group of Jews who probably weren't going to like what he had to say. He knew how many other Jews had reacted to his message, and the physical and emotional toll of what was to come was weighing on him. Seeing fellow believers before having to confront a hostile crowd gave Paul the courage he needed in that moment.

Being an advocate for the gospel and facing so much opposition can wear on a person—even a person as impressive as Paul. God knew Paul needed some encouragement, and He placed the right people at the right time to do just that. Our fellow brothers and sisters in Christ are gifts from God for our spiritual growth. None of us were called to live out the Christian faith on our own. We are called to join a body of believers to work together (see 1 Cor. 12). And like Paul, we should thank God for each of them.

delight |

What do you think it was like for Paul's mental and emotional state to see friends at this point of his ministry?

What impact do your friends have on you and your faith?

Presence and Purpose

display |

Consider how you see your brothers and sisters in Christ. Begin observing their actions and behaviors. When you see someone looking as though they are discouraged or upset, try to comfort them. Do your best to be understanding of what they may be going through and be present with them in their pain. There will always be days when we are dreading something, but it is so much easier to move forward if we have a friend to cheer us on.

Name a girl who you can seek to encourage through a difficult time today. Lift her up to God in prayer, asking Him for an opportunity to cross paths today.

Thank God for the Christian friends in your life. Name them individually and say one thing you appreciate about them. If you feel you need some Christian friends, then talk to God about it. Ask God to make you a good friend to others. Talk to Him about ways you want to be an encouragement to others but may be afraid of rejection.

Come On Over

discover |

Paul stayed two whole years in his own rented house. And he welcomed all who visited him, proclaiming the kingdom of God and teaching about the Lord Jesus Christ with all boldness and without hindrance.

When you think of following Jesus, what comes to mind? Perhaps you think of living a morally virtuous life—doing and saying all the right things, staying pure, going to church, singing Christian hymns or praise songs, praying, and reading your Bible. But what about welcoming people into your home and sharing meals with them? Did that come to mind?

The book of Acts wraps up with a description of how Paul spent his time in Rome, and one of the things he did most often was simply welcome people into his home. Luke, the author of Acts, doesn't explicitly say that Paul shared meals with those he welcomed, but we can assume he did, as that was the common custom of his day when inviting someone into your home. This tells us that ministry isn't as complicated or as intimidating as we sometimes make it out to be. A big part of spreading the gospel is simply hanging out with people, sharing a meal, and simply getting to know them. You don't have to preach on street corners or from a stage if you want to be a part of spreading the good news of Jesus and the kingdom of God. You can start by simply going to lunch with a friend or inviting someone to eat with you and your family. There is no wrong time to share the good news about Jesus with others, but sharing this news over a meal with friends is certainly one of the most effective.

Presence and Purpose

delight |

What sorts of things did Paul do while he was in Rome? What can you learn from his example?

Paul regularly welcomed people into his home. How could you be more welcoming to girls around you who don't know Jesus? Why is this an important part of following Jesus?

display |

Take a moment to consider a girl you know who doesn't know Jesus who you could build a closer relationship with this week. How could you deepen your friendship with her? Perhaps you could send her an encouraging note or invite her to hang out with you and your friends, or maybe it could be as simple as asking how she's doing. Don't worry about what you will say or even about making sure you say the right things. Ministry often starts with simply showing up and striving to be a good friend to the people around you.

Thank God for welcoming you into His family through faith in Jesus. Ask Him to help you be a more welcoming person to the people around you. Pray that God would help you see the people around you who you could be a better friend or neighbor to as a means of pointing them toward Jesus.

The Times of the Acts

It's fair to say a lot happened in the book of Acts, but it can be difficult for us today to determine exactly how much time passed over the course of these 28 chapters. To get a handle on when things we've studied happened (and to help us review), fill in the following timeline. First, take a colored pen or fine-tipped marker and write out the number of the devotion day that applies to each Scripture. Then, come up with a news headline for what happened in that chapter. (Use your devotion as a guide!)

Acts 1 (AD 30)

What happened?

Acts 8 (AD 35)

What happened?

Acts 2 (AD 30)

What happened?

Acts 9 (AD 36)

What happened?

Acts 4 (AD 35)

What happened?

Acts 10 (AD 40)

What happened?

Acts 5 (AD 35)

What happened?

Acts 11 (AD 43)

What happened?

Acts 7 (AD 35)

What happened?

Acts 12 (AD 45)

What happened?

Acts 13 (AD 47-48)

What happened?

Acts 21 (AD 54, 58)

What happened?

Acts 14 (AD 48)

What happened?

Acts 23 (AD 59)

What happened?

Acts 15 (AD 50-51)

What happened?

Acts 24 (AD 59)

What happened?

Acts 16 (AD 51)

What happened?

Acts 25 (AD 59)

What happened?

Acts 18 (AD 51, 54)

What happened?

Acts 26 (AD 59)

What happened?

Acts 19 (AD 54)

What happened?

Acts 27 (AD 60)

What happened?

Acts 20 (AD 54)

What happened?

Acts 28 (AD 61-62)

What happened?

All Things for Good

When we read about Jesus's life—especially how He was innocent, yet crucified as if He were guilty—maybe we shake our heads and think, "That doesn't seem just." Then, when we move into the book of Acts and see what happened to the apostles, we think, "That doesn't seem fair." And the truth is, whether these things seem fair or just or not, they were a vital part of God's plan. Let's break down a few passages to see the many ways God took bad things and used them for good. Use these three questions to guide your answer: **what happened, what's your initial reaction, and how did God use the situation for good?**

Acts 4.

Acts 5:17-42.

Acts 7:54-60.

Acts 9.

Acts 12.

Acts 14:18-20.

Acts 16.

Acts 19:21-41.

Acts 22:22-30.

Now, think about when you have faced persecution or difficulty because of your faith. Using the same three questions, choose a specific situation and see how God used (or is using) that for good.

Sources

1. "Acts and the Epistles Chronology - Study Resources," Blue Letter Bible, accessed January 13, 2022, https://www.blueletterbible.org/study/pnt/pnt02.cfm.; Stanley E. Porter, "Acts," in *CSB Study Bible*, ed. Edwin A. Blum and Trevin Wax (Nashville, TN: Holman Bible Publishers, 2017), 1714.